THE
UNGLOBALS

The Unglobals

Groundbreakers in the Age of Economic Nationalism

J. Mark Munoz

UNION BRIDGE BOOKS
An imprint of Wimbledon Publishing Company Limited (WPC)

UNION BRIDGE BOOKS
75–76 Blackfriars Road
London SE1 8HA

www.unionbridgebooks.com

British Library Cataloguing-in-Publication Data
A catalogue record for this book is available from the British Library.

ISBN-13: 978-1-78527-055-0 (Hbk)
ISBN-10: 1-78527-055-9 (Hbk)

This title is also available as an e-book.

This book is dedicated to my parents, Jose Edgar Munoz and Charity Judith Munoz. Hope it inspires you and many others around the world.

CONTENTS

ILLUSTRATIONS

Figure

Tables

1

THE WORLD IS NOT THAT FLAT

The world is truly integrated. Countries, companies and individuals worldwide are all happy. Everyone is winning, right?

Unfortunately, as many of us already know, this is not the current reality. There are winners and losers in our globalized society. While some have reaped the rewards, billions of people have been left behind and continue to live in desperation and poverty. In fact, a World Bank report indicated that about 10 percent of the world population, or 767 million people, lived on less than $1.90 per day (World Bank, 2016).

Millions are leaving their countries to find better lives elsewhere. A United Nations High Commissioner for Refugees (2017) report indicated that there are about 22.5 million refugees, and that approximately 28,300 people each day are forced to leave their homes as a result of conflict and persecution.

In a 2017 Pew *Global Report*, it was noted that 72 percent of people in Venezuela, 68 percent in Mexico and 57 percent in Jordan felt that life was worse for them now than what it was 50 years ago (Poushter, 2017).

Disparities in trade exist among nations. For instance, about half of globally traded goods (e.g., office equipment) come from emerging countries, while in other sectors (e.g., pharmaceutical industries) developed nations continue to lead (Bertelsmann Stiftung, 2016).

Many companies have not really optimized global participation. In fact, in the United States, the majority of small and medium enterprises do not export, and less than 1 percent of about 30 million firms in the country sell abroad (Pinkus, Manyika and Ramaswany, 2017).

Executives worldwide are aware of the unevenness brought about by globalization. In a PWC (2017) survey of CEOs, 44 percent indicated that globalization has not helped seal the gap between rich and poor.

In the United States and the United Kingdom, news stories with the word "globalization" have taken a negative tone due to pressures against globalization in these countries (Ghemawat, 2017). Populist leanings have been evident with the emergence of the "America First" phenomenon and Britain's exit from the European Union, or "Brexit."

Negative viewpoints are evident in other countries as well. Reports show that discontentment with globalization has been prevalent. In a YouGov (2016) survey approximately 78 percent of Indonesians, 57 percent of Indians, 53 percent of Filipinos and 52 percent of the French people felt that their country could meet its needs without relying on importations from other nations. In various media around the world, stories of countries taking on populist, protectionist and even isolationist standpoints have become common.

There has been a rise in consumer ethnocentrism and economic nationalism. Trade and globalization have been identified as the cause for job losses (Pinkus, Manyika and

Ramaswamy, 2017). There are populist politicians who allude to free trade and job outsourcing to other nations as the primary cause for problems in their countries (Tomita, 2017).

New ideologies are emerging. For instance, support for alter-globalization has been on the rise. The movement aims to address negative globalization consequences relating to economic, political, cultural, social and environmental issues.

The reality is, globalization is uneven and oftentimes unfair. The world is "flat," linked and highly progressive in certain spots. However, in other locations geography, culture, politics and economics continue to stall growth and development. Antiglobalization movements have grown as a result of income disparities between the rich and the poor, immigration and job competition (Tomita, 2017).

In many parts of the world "barriers" and "walls" and "impregnable terrain" continue to hinder economic socialization. There are still several poorly developed cities all over the world with lack of access to basic utilities and infrastructure. In Eritrea, there are only six cell phone subscriptions per 100 people (World Atlas, 2017). This is the lowest cell phone subscription base in the world. This situation limits the country's ability to connect with the rest of the world. In fact, in West Africa, only about 18 percent of roads are paved (Dahir, 2017), thereby limiting mobility of people and trade.

Many countries such as Greece, North Korea, Venezuela, Yemen, Burundi, the Central African Republic and the Democratic Republic of Congo face tough economic and political challenges. The *Economist* (2017) listed South Sudan as the most miserable country in 2018 with inflation above 150 percent, conflict between army and tribal militia and about 1.7 million people facing famine.

International macroeconomic volatility has led to fear and uncertainty in the global community. The past financial crisis is a reminder that economic conditions and events in one country can spread globally like wildfire. A World Economic Forum (2017a) report cited financial crises and the failure of financial mechanisms or institutions as notable global risk factors. The 2008 financial crisis cost the US economy over $22 trillion (Melendez, 2013).

Within our global society, however, the notion of "global citizenship" applies to many, but not everyone. Global exclusion has been rampant. The children working in mines in Africa, young farmers in remote villages in Vietnam and the street vendors in India are detached from many opportunities brought about by globalization. Their chance to be "global citizens" is not impossible, but highly limited.

Everyday, the rest of the world goes through the daily grind, struggling to cope with and survive the mounting pressure brought by globalization. With intensifying competition, executives are trying to outthink and outwork others. Executives in some countries hardly take vacations. In Japan, executives took only five vacation days, in South Korea they took seven and in the United States they took ten (Polland, 2012). The number was significantly lower than the total vacation days they were entitled to. In Japan, a young journalist was reported to have died of heart failure due to overwork. She did 159 hours of overtime work in one month (*The Guardian*, 2017).

In all corners of the world, technological enhancements have meant convenient access to work 24/7. In an HR

Certification Institute (2017) survey it was found that 17 percent of executives always work while on vacation, and that 59 percent occasionally work when on vacation.

Many executives are constantly online and are constantly chasing work or pleasure. In fact, an average person spends more amount of time on their computer and phone than sleeping. Typical sleeping time for an average person is 8 hours and 21 minutes, while the average time spent on media devices is 8 hours and 41 minutes (Davies, 2015).

For many, life balance has been skewed. In order to win in the ultracompetitive global game, executives have blurred the lines separating work and life. As a consequence, relationships, health and happiness have been compromised.

While many are caught up in a global game of survival, there are people who do not even know what globalization is and simply do not care. Regardless of whether it was a result of personal choice or life situation, some have become detached from the global rat race.

This book does not engage in the globalization blame game. There are too many underlying factors and flawed systems to consider. Instead of spending time griping and trying to understand the reasons behind the failures of globalization and society, this very short book takes a different approach. It focuses on what one should do about it.

The intent is to reach the busy global populace who have started to wonder, "Is this hectic and stressful work pace the way I want to live the rest of my life?" The book was intentionally designed to be brief. With easy Web connectivity, and mobile and social media platforms available, who has time to read a long book?

The author's intent is to encourage a pause from life and some introspection. After reading this book, I would urge readers to contemplate these important questions: *How should you live your life in this complex and challenging global environment? How can you find personal peace and happiness? How can you manage the changes brought about by growing economic nationalism?*

This book consists of three concise chapters. The present chapter, 1, highlights five fictional stories of people who managed to detach themselves from globalization. For the purpose of convenience, they are called the unglobals. Chapter 2 analyzes and discusses the mindset of the unglobals. Chapter 3 outlines considerations relating to alternative pathways for organizational and personal success in an era of economic nationalism.

The following pages feature fictional but plausible stories of five unglobals. The stories are designed to entertain, but more importantly to showcase key lessons that can change one's life and to identify transformational pathways in a complex, global world.

Alex, Former Export–Import Executive

"Did you see the latest bill on the table?" Anna yelled, half-mockingly, half-annoyed.

"Yes," Alex responded softly as he gazed at the bills piling up on the table. Tears welled up in his eyes. Sadness and desperation. When will this ever end? he asked himself.

His mind briefly drifted to the glory days not too long ago. He had successfully built his vitamin company, importing vitamins from Australia and Brazil and marketing them in the United States and Canada. Business was brisk, and he was on track to becoming a multimillionaire.

"Globalization stinks," he thought. Just as his business had started to pick up, foreign competitors from China and South Korea entered the market, first eroding his margins, then pushing him to the brink of bankruptcy.

"Things happen so fast," he mumbled. Was it just a few months ago when business was booming? "How could my business shift from hero to zero in a few months?" he wondered.

And, oh his marriage. How can women be so fickle-minded? Anna, his fiancée, showered him with love and affection when things were great. Now all he got were glaring, disappointed looks and countless insults. And, the yelling. How he hated it! A woman yelling at you day and night can drive you crazy. This has got to stop, he thought. This relationship was toxic and detrimental to his mental and physical health.

He picked up the phone and dialed Bill Harris's number from memory. Bill was his high school buddy and best friend. Bill was a successful lawyer and always seemed to make the right choices in life. Alex made it a point to call Bill and get his opinion when important decisions had to be made. Plus, his legal insight could prevent potential lawsuits.

"Bill, I need your advice."

"I'm all ears, buddy. What's going on?"

"What are the legal consequences if I just disappeared? Dead silence.

"You're not planning to kill yourself are you?" Bill was aware of Alex's personal and professional troubles and knew he was constantly depressed.

"No … no … nothing like that. I mean selling the house, the business and all my possessions, and just live off the grid. Like in a cave."

Bill laughed. "C'mon, you can't be serious?"

"I am. I really am! I'm sick and tired of this, Bill. Can't take this anymore. I just want to simplify my life. Get rid of this mental baggage and just live simply in a cave. You know, like homesteaders. We've seen some of those shows on television. Those people live simply. They have less complex lives and are a lot happier. Just simple happiness."

"You don't know squat about that kind of life. Look at you, you're as cosmopolitan as it gets," Bill argued.

"Trade-offs, Bill. I'll have to do trade-offs. It's a choice—take on a stressful urban life that's a rat race or live through self-sustenance in the hills somewhere." Alex paused and gave the matter some added thought, "You know I'm a fast learner. I'll read up on the topic and develop a plan."

"I'm not totally against it. We all need to find what makes us happy. Those homesteaders in Alaska we saw on television did seem happy. Just want to make you think through this carefully. Plan well. Not much legal complication here. Just make sure you cover all your debts. Start a new life completely debt free."

"Thanks, bud."

"Sure thing. Let me know how things progress. What's your timeline for this?"

"About three months."

"That soon, huh?"

"Yep. Things tend to happen quickly around here."

"And Anna?"

"Who? I'm done with her. Besides, I'm sure she wouldn't want to go where I'm going. I may just hook up with a local or keep a bear for a companion."

They both laughed. Alex smiled. For the first time in recent months, he felt a semblance of joy and hope.

Five months later, Alex had completed his humble cave home on a secluded property in Montana. After having sold all of his possessions, he had about $35,000 left. He used the money to buy a small property with a cave on the premises. He did some of the construction on the cave himself, but sought the help of a local contractor for the solar panel and compost bathroom. He bought a shotgun for hunting and protection.

He was not too far from a lake. He bought fishing supplies to catch and store fish.

His "cave house" was modest but comfortable. He was proud that it was completely environment-friendly.

He got himself a dog to keep him company. Bud was a two-year-old Lab mix that he picked up from a local shelter. He figured Bud could join him during hunting and keep an ear out for wandering predators at night.

He never felt happier and freer. He no longer had to live for money. He was off the pressure of an urban life-style. In fact, he was mostly cut off from the world. He didn't even have a phone or television.

He picked up hundreds of junked and very old books. He read them for entertainment and to keep his mind sharp.

Food had never been an issue. He hunted and gathered food. He did odd jobs here and there to buy canned food for the winter.

After six months as a homesteader, he decided to celebrate. He set a campfire outside the cave and enjoyed the view of the mountains as sunset approached. He had bought a six-pack of beer earlier in the week. He took a sip from the first bottle. It wasn't cold. But, hey, he thought, it was all about trade-offs. He thought about his past life and his past frustrations. Did he make the right call to live as a homesteader?

He looked at Bud, who was beside him watching the fire. "Did we make the right call, Bud? I think we did."

The adjustment process was rough. He missed many of the conveniences of his past life—the television, the microwave, the washing machine, the Internet. Hunting and fishing could be frustrating at times. It took a lot of time and effort to catch anything. But he learned to adjust. In recent months, he had become a much better hunter. He became a farmer too and planted simple crops like beets, carrots, lettuce, pumpkins and tomatoes. He also started to raise chickens and sheep. He had started to read books on fishing and food preservation.

He was a changed man, and a happier one.

He took a long sip from his second bottle of beer. He thought to himself, "Why didn't I think of this earlier in life?"

John, Tech Consultant

It was 7:00 p.m. at the Brown household.

As a tech consultant, John Brown was a very busy man. On this day, he arrived home at around 6:00 p.m. He turned on his home computer and started answering e-mails and responding to voice messages.

It was now 7:00 p.m., and there was no dinner on the table. His wife, Agnes, an advertising executive, was on the phone texting clients.

John's 13-year-old daughter, Sally, was also on her mobile phone playing a game in the corner of the family room. Sam, his 11-year-old son was watching a YouTube video on his phone.

This had been a routine almost every night. The family hardly had time to talk. Within the next 30 minutes, everyone would fix themselves a ham and cheese sandwich while on their phones. Then, they would go to their respective rooms.

John looked at his family. This didn't seem right. While he was a lover of the power of technology and how it brought the world together in a faster, cheaper and oftentimes meaningful way, he detested the decline in human interaction. He was seeing this happen in his family. In fact, he had seen it everywhere—workplaces, malls, social gatherings, hospitals, funerals and even in church. He jokingly called it "hyperphonism"—overindulgence on mobile phones. Some people John knew had been afflicted with "nomophobia"—fear of being separated from a mobile device or "no-mobile-phobia."

John loved his mobile phone. This morning he was raving at the fact that his mobile device allowed him to speak with colleagues in four continents at the same time—one in Europe, one in Asia, one in South America and one in Africa. He led the call via Skype on his mobile phone in Michigan, United States, while walking to his office from the parking area.

Technology certainly got you globally connected. But was there a price to pay?

He stood up from his office table in the family room and blurted out, "Hey, guys, we have to talk!"

Agnes was on the phone and signaled that she'd be done in a minute.

The kids ignored him.

"Everyone, we need to talk now!" he yelled loudly.

That got everyone's attention.

"Let's gather around the dinner table. I ordered pizza and chicken wings for dinner. It will be here shortly. But, before we eat as a family, let's talk."

Everyone gathered at the dinner table, hesitantly. They were all curious about what was going on. This was certainly out of the routine.

John looked at all of them and said softly, "We're all so engrossed with our mobile devices that we're not talking as a family."

Sally blurted out, "That's not true, I text mom all the time!"

John looked at her, "Exactly—we're all just texting each other, and no one does actual talking anymore. One time your mom even texted me from bed to tell me that she was going to the bathroom!"

Agnes blurted out, "I did not."

John responded, smiling, "Yes, you did. A couple of weeks ago. I saved it."

The family looked at him, wondering what he was really up to.

John continued, "Look, guys, when I was growing up, we were busy too. Your grandfather worked ten to twelve hours each day on the farm. Your grandmother taught part-time while managing the household. I helped on the farm while studying. But, we always spent dinner together every night. We shared stories and ideas. We laughed and cried together. We were socially connected as a family. We've developed a very strong bond. I'm concerned we'll lose that bond now with so little social interaction."

Agnes chimed in, "John, we're a close family. You all know we love each other a lot and look after each other."

John responded, "I know that, but I feel this mobile technology is causing us all to drift apart."

Sam looked at John, "What do you suggest we do, Dad?"

"How about we try to find some balance? How about we have technology days? You can use your mobile device around the house on Tuesday, Thursday and Saturday. The rest of the days it will be turned off and stored, and we'll all just hang around and talk as a family. What do you think?"

Sally said, "But, Dad, I have group text with friends every day at 5:00 p.m. If I don't join these sessions, they'll likely talk about me!"

"If they are really your friends, they'll understand our family's rules."

Agnes nodded, "I think your dad's request sounds reasonable. We're all addicted to phones, including your dad. It will take some serious adjustment by all of us, but it may do some good for all of us. For example, Sally, how about you and I cook dinner together on the no-tech days? John, you and Sam can play ball for an hour. When was the last time you guys played ball?

John's face reddened, "It's been awhile. Yes, let's all do some fun stuff on no-tech days. What do you say, guys? All in?"

"I guess I'm in." Sally says.

Sam jumped in, "Me too!"

The doorbell rang. Dinner had arrived.

After six months, John noticed the change in his family. They definitely had bonded better and had become closer. With heightened interaction, they found new things to do together. For instance, while playing ball with Sam the other day, Sam told him about a movie he wanted to watch. Over dinner, he learned that Sally wanted to watch it too. So, the whole family was going watch the movie together on the coming weekend. The initial conversation about the movie would not have happened via text message.

While thinking about the movie, John was pacing in the hallway by the office of George Brando, the vice president of operations of the tech firm he worked for. He was anxious. He was going to pitch a radical idea to George, and he wasn't sure how George would take it. He worried he might look like some kind of loony. But, he believed in the idea. "No guts, no glory," he thought.

The secretary stepped out into the hallway. "You can come in now, John," she said, with a big smile.

George stood up to shake John's hand, "How are you, John?"

"I've been well, George, and you?"

"Fine. Actually not too fine—after just reviewing the tech upgrade budget we need to spend on." George pored over a pile of papers in his desk and started to rearrange them. "What is it that you want to discuss?"

John's palms were sweating. George was very direct and blunt, and had taken the skill of peer humiliation to an art form. His tirades and insults had been legendary and could be a career wrecker. If you ended up in his wrong side, you'd be the butt of corporate jokes for several years.

"George, I'd like to run an idea by you. It's just an idea, it may even be half crazy. But I tested it with my family, and it seems to be working. I'm wondering whether it might be replicable in our workplace."

George stared at him, "Tell me more."

John took a deep breath. "I noticed in my household that we hardly talked. Everyone was caught up with their tech devices. I implemented what I called no-tech days where everyone does not use the cell phone and instead we do activities together and find ways to bond more. In my home, we decided on Tuesday, Thursday and Saturday. We actually got close and ..."

"Stop!" George interrupted.

John braced himself for a tirade.

George looked at him intently, "I love it! I'd like to do the same at my home, and, heck, I'd love to see the same in the office. We can all bond better. We're not the same firm we were ten years ago. Everyone seems colder, more engrossed. We need to get along better."

John was amazed, "You like it. Seriously?"

George looked at him incredulously, "Of course, I do. It's brilliant. I'm not a fan of this tech stuff. I believe in people, and the power of teams. I bet your idea will improve morale and productivity, and may even save us some money on phone bills. Take the lead in this initiative. Let's have Tuesday and Thursday as 'no-tech' days. Make it happen."

John was excited. "I was also thinking about the possibility of having Friday as a "local" day. We've become so engrossed in going global in recent years that I feel we don't get to interact as much with our counterparts in other states. Perhaps, the local day—once a week—would allow us to strengthen relationships and enhance collaboration with other local offices?

George smiled, "Where the hell are you getting these great ideas? Love this one too!"

John responded, "Honestly? I've tried to limit tech use to two days a week myself. In the process, I've been generating a lot of new ideas."

In the next few months, John implemented the "no-tech" and "local" days in the company. He collaborated closely with all departments. As George predicted, morale and productivity improved, and cost reductions were noted.

John also just moved to a new office. Outside the door a sign read, John Brown, Assistant Vice President of Operations.

Ismael, Deep-Sea Diver

The sun was just about to rise by the Sulu Sea in the Philippines.

Every day, by the crack of dawn, Ismael, a member of a local Badjao tribe, paddled his small canoe toward the deep sea.

He was thin and dark, the end result of countless days of hard work in the ocean throughout his 15 years of life.

He coughed and spat into the water. The cool morning air sometimes caused his throat to itch, or was it the heavy ingestion of salt water? He didn't know, and didn't really care.

Today, like any other day, he had an important mission. He had to dive for deep-sea pearls that he could sell to local traders. Yesterday, he didn't do too well. He only got two small pieces. He needed to get six to make it worth his while. The money he earned from the sale of the pearls, allowed him to buy food for his family. He was the breadwinner in the family. His father had perished at sea several years ago. He made it a point to fend for himself; his mother, Suburan; and his nine-year-old brother, Sakur. Everyone in the family made an effort to help them to survive. Suburan sold fish in the market, and Sakur gathered seaweed and shells by the shore to add to their meals. Sakur was too young to go deep-sea diving with him.

As he paddled his canoe, he wondered about his future. Would he be doing this same thing the rest of life like his father? At what point would he perish like his dad? His was a tough life. He sometimes envied those other island boys who went to school every day. In a few years, they would have jobs and wouldn't have to work as hard as he did.

Ismael scratched his sunburned skin. Those pesky jellyfish, he thought. He hated the itch they caused. The itch could sometimes stay for days. "Do they have medication to ease these bites?" he wondered. But even if there was one, he probably couldn't afford it. The money would be better spent on food for the family.

When could he ever score a giant pearl? His neighbor Boyet once found a very large pearl and sold it for a lot of money. He was able to build a small house from the sale. Ismael wished he could find a pearl like that one day.

God knew their house could use some repair or, better yet, total rebuilding.

His stomach growled. He was hungry. His last meal was lunch yesterday. He had had no dinner or breakfast. Such was their way of life. Eat when you can. He was accustomed to it. He'd survive.

The key thing was to find the energy and stamina today to dive 20, 30 and maybe 50 feet to get hold of those black sea pearls.

He wished he had that sophisticated diving gear he'd seen foreigners use once. That equipment made diving very easy. He smiled, those guys are wimps though. If he had that equipment, he would likely be able to get lots of pearls. He wondered how much that diving equipment cost?

He stopped rowing his canoe. This might be good spot, he thought. He threw out his makeshift anchor, put on his goggles and jumped into the water.

The water was warm and sparking blue. He strained his eyes for large oysters. He dove deeper and deeper and deeper. He found a small one and placed it in his diving bag. He found another one and did the same. He wanted to check out one more site but suddenly felt the extreme need for air. How long was he in the water? He didn't bother to time himself. When it was time to go up, it was time to go up. He surfaced and gasped for air. He loaded the bag contents in his canoe and aimed to dive into his new target spot. This time he got three. This was a good day, thus far.

He dove one more time, and a large oyster far ahead caught his eye. Could he make it? It seemed so far away. Was it 50 feet? He'd never ventured that deep. He could hear his father's voice, "Never venture beyond 50 feet unless you're ready. It takes many years of practice."

How many years had he practiced? Was he ready? He wondered. He decided to make a go for it. He dove and inched closer to the large oyster. It was farther than he expected. Was it 60 or 70 feet? He wanted to give up, but thought, "I can't give up now! I'm so close!"

His lungs were screaming for air. He felt he was about to pass out. But, the oyster was within reach. It was large. He needed two hands to carry it to the top. Could he even carry it? It looked heavy. Adrenaline kicked in. He grabbed the large oyster and took it up. It's now or never, he thought. I'll do this even if I have to die trying. He wondered if this was what had happened to his dad. His mustered all his strength and propelled upward. A large shark trailed him. His life flashed through his mind. He continued thrusting upward and miraculously made it to the surface. He dumped the oyster in the canoe and jumped in.

The shark missed him by just a few inches.

Ismael gasped for breath. His head was pounding, and he felt nauseous. He crept alongside the large oyster, embraced it and drifted into sleep.

He passed out for hours. But, eventually woke up feeling somewhat better. He started to feel cold, though, feeling a strong gust of wind.

Dark clouds loomed on the horizon, and rain started to pour. He had to head back home immediately. His small canoe was not designed to withstand a storm.

He paddled the canoe like a madman. I have to get home now! I'd love to show this oyster to mother. This could change our lives forever.

It took hours of ferocious paddling, but eventually the coastal village was in sight. He started to pace his strokes. It was getting dark, but home was near.

He brought the canoe to shore and walked toward his family's dilapidated shack.

His mom, Suburan, was cooking the usual dinner of fish and rice. Sakur was skinning some fish in the corner.

Ismael walked in quietly, hardly able to contain his excitement. "Mother," he said, "I found the biggest oyster ever!"

He showed the oyster to Suburan. She gasped. "Huh? How did you get it? It must have been so deep!"

He knew how his mother felt about risk taking. He had heard her warnings almost everyday for years. "It was not so deep, Mother," he lied.

Suburan smiled excitedly, "Well, let's take a look at it!"

The family gathered in a small table. Suburan helped Ismael open the oyster with a kitchen knife. It took a significant effort.

Finally, the shell cracked open, and the largest black pearl they had seen in their lives came into view. They all gasped.

The pearl's brilliance and beauty were magnified by the nearby candle.

The family sat speechless and in awe. They knew their lives would be forever changed for the better. Ismael slowly pulled Suburan and Sakur close to him and gave them a big hug. Tears of joy rolled from their eyes.

Six months later, the family had a new life. The pearl was sold for $50,000 to a local trader. It was the largest commercial sale in history of the village. Suburan now owned a small grocery store. Their house was the best looking in the village. Ismael owned a fleet of ten large canoes. He directed the entire team of pearl divers in the village. He was on track to becoming the wealthiest young man in the village. They even had a name for him, "Datu Mussah" or "The King of Pearl."

Jose and Maria, Estate Caretakers

In a remote village in rural Spain, the sun showed its magnificence by rising through a corner of a large mountain crevice, cascading its rays into the isolated valleys.

The view of the sun rising through the steep mountains was a sight that an elderly couple, Jose and Maria, was accustomed to viewing every day. They watched the sunrise while sipping coffee on the deck by their home.

Well, it was not technically their home or even their deck. They were caretakers of an old castle in ruins. They had been hired as caretakers by the government's historical society.

They kept the place nice and clean. In exchange, food, medical and cleaning supplies were transported to them every three months.

The nearest village was over a thousand kilometers away. Jose and Maria only got to see another human being once a quarter.

They were accustomed to this life of isolation and enjoyed it. They took pride in their work as custodians of history. Even in their early 70s, they lived an active life. They kept the castle spotlessly clean. They felt it was their moral obligation to their country and to the world. They viewed their work as a small but meaningful contribution.

Jose and Maria liked to plan ahead. Given their remote location, they planted various crops and raised farm animals on the property to have provisions in case the food supplies didn't arrive on time. From their calculations, they could survive for a year without delivered provisions.

They were also very particular about environmental conservation. They kept waste to a minimum and recycled where they could. They had a small solar system getup to help with some of their energy needs. They believed that more important than historical property, conservation was the preservation of Mother Earth.

As they were sipping coffee and watching the sunrise, Jose mumbled softly, "I'll have to get fresh water from the spring today."

It was not his favorite chore. He'd have to connect two large buckets to a six-foot pole and fill the buckets up with spring water. He'd have to make two or three trips today. The fresh supply would cover all their needs for a few days. Fortunately, the spring was just a few hundred meters away.

Maria looked at him emphatically, "Do you think it might rain? I see some dark clouds on the horizon. We should probably put out our water basins and catch some of the rain water."

Jose nodded and smiled, "We probably should. It could save me a trip or two to the well."

Funny, he thought, that in a place like this, we simply pick up the information we need and use it right away. We don't have to sift through hundreds or thousands of pieces of information to understand what's going on and make a decision. Here we gather what we can from the environment and make a judgment call. It kept life simple and made him more productive.

Jose and Maria didn't see people often. With the nearest village so far away, they received practically no news from the outside world. Terms like terrorism, financial crisis, civil wars, drought and famine meant nothing to them. Occasionally, news from the outside world was delivered by Felipe, who traveled to visit them on horseback and with a carriage full of supplies. They saw him once every three or four months. Felipe told them a lot of interesting stories. Most of the stories were meaningless to them and often laughable. For example, why would a country elect a dictator? Why would a political group espouse violence to gain peace? Why would people spend most of their time facing a computer or a mobile phone? None of these actions made sense to them. This news simply made Jose feel lucky that he lived in semi-isolation.

He remembered a disturbing conversation he had had with Felipe during his last visit.

"What's this world coming to, Senor Jose?" Felipe had said.

"What do you mean?" Jose was puzzled.

"My cousin Eduardo was injured in the recent terrorist attack in Barcelona. He was one in over a hundred injured, and several people died." Felipe looked very dejected.

Jose looked at him sadly. "What happened?"

"Well," Felipe stammered, as if unsure of what to say or where to start. "It was a terrorist attack. A terrorist took a van and ran over people."

Jose was confused, "Why would someone do something like that?"

Felipe looked stumped. "I don't really know. The van driver was allegedly a member of an organization called the Islamic State of Iraq and Syria, or ISIS. The group undertakes religious violence to advance its ideology."

Jose shook his head, "How sad it is that so many were injured, including your cousin Eduardo. I hope he gets better soon. With all the technology and information available, no one saw this coming?"

Felipe merely shook his head.

Jose looked at Felipe sadly. "Perhaps, information and technology can be leveraged better to help others. Perhaps it can be used to enhance understanding and to find peace."

Jose remembered how relieved he felt then that he was far away from any potential violence. He couldn't shake the memory of Felipe's face that day. Felipe had the look of a distraught man who was facing fear and sorrow. Jose didn't want to be in that world.

The story led to some concerns, though.

The truth is that he needed Felipe and the government to be well and functional. The government provided supplies that were not critical to his survival, but were helpful. The canned food, medicines, toiletries, cleaning supplies, tools and batteries added much comfort to his life. He was glad the government never forgot them. Sometimes the supplies arrived late, but they always arrived at some point.

Felipe had been diligent, hardworking and reliable. It was a major sacrifice for him to travel so far on horseback to deliver the supplies.

Jose often wondered why Felipe gleefully presented him with old magazines and newspapers. The information shown on those pages was irrelevant to him. The advertised clothes were things he would never, ever wear. He would never own that advertised home furniture. He was clueless about the technology gadgets. He found some use for newspapers, though. They came handy whenever he built a fire. He found it polite not to say anything negative about it to Felipe. The old magazines and newspapers kept coming.

What he appreciated most from Felipe's visits were the books he brought. Jose frequently requested copies of books. He enjoyed reading books about farming, raising animals and wilderness survival. He reads very few books, and the few he did read were targeted toward the development of a specific skill or knowledge. He jokingly called it "precision information."

Maria rose from the table and deposited her coffee cup in the kitchen sink. She left Jose on the patio, letting him wander with his own thoughts. She'd spend the next hour or so double-checking their batteries, especially, the ones for the satellite phone. This was an important piece of equipment for them, one that could potentially save their lives during a natural disaster or medical emergency. With their isolated lifestyle, meticulous planning and strategic thinking were key.

Just as she completed all her chores, Maria noticed Jose arriving with the two large buckets of fresh water.

He was panting. He struggled with the weight of the load. She held the door open for him to ease his entry into the old castle.

"*Dios Mio!*" he gasped. "This load seems to be getting heavier every time."

Maria looked at her husband emphatically. "Don't worry, dear. You don't have to fetch any more water in the next few days. I'm sure it will rain soon. I have all the water basins out and ready."

He looked at his wife in a grateful and amused fashion. How lucky he was to have her. Over the years, she has developed a whole range of skills, ranging from cooking, to sewing, to farming, to animal raising, to bee keeping, to house cleaning, and it looked like she could now add weather forecasting to the already impressive list.

The rain started to pour heavily. Again, she was right. They'd have to work indoors today. But, they would definitely have time for a nap. He gave the matter some thought and smiled. What a job they had! They worked all the time but could take a nap anytime.

Ecuador Mountain Women

Agnes, the head of the women's craft association, flicked at the fly buzzing by her face. She was annoyed—not just at the fly but also at the state they were in. Their organization consisted of 50 women from a remote mountain village in Ecuador.

Their primary livelihood was the creation of embroidered crafts for clothing and housewares. Their crafts were tastefully made and would be suited for the most fashionable women and the finest homes.

Yet, no one knew about them. Few bought their products.

Their families lived in poverty, and the community was desperate for change.

They wanted to market their goods to the world, but did not have the know-how, network or resources to make it happen. There were a few futile attempts in the past.

Their craft lacked sustainability and faced future extinction. Many of the younger women no longer wished to be involved in embroidery. They preferred better-paying jobs in the bigger cities.

Lourdes, one of the more vocal women, raised her voice, "We have to stop this exodus of our young women."

Agnes countered, "We can't tell them what to do. This is a free country. They can do as they please. I'd love to have them stay, but we have to find another way to get them engaged. We certainly can't forbid them to leave."

Milagros, one of the largest producers, chimed in, "How about we engage them with activities the youth of today want to do? Use social media like Facebook and Twitter. We can also show our work through YouTube."

Agnes nodded, "We've talked about a website several times. Maybe now is the time to do it through our youth."

Lourdes countered "What do we pay them with?"

Agnes flicked at a fly again, "We can offer them a commission for every sale. Whoever creates the website gets a sales percentage. Whoever sells though their blogs or video blogs also earns. There can be several income streams for everyone."

Milagros added excitedly, "Maybe the local cooperative can provide a small start-up capital for them."

Agnes smiled, "Certainly a possibility."

In the next few months, their craft organization lobbied with local government officials, private companies and local communities to support a campaign they called "*Ciudad Fuerte*," or strong town. They implemented a domestically focused marketing campaign anchored on cultural preservation, job creation and unity. They utilized all marketing tools at their disposal: social media, Internet ads, word-of-mouth advertising, print ads, billboards, flyers, press releases, event sponsorships and public relations campaigns. They were able to raise thousands of dollars in private donations.

One early dawn, as Agnes stepped out of her house, she heard giggling noises on a neighbor's patio. She was surprised to find six teenage girls busy creating billboards and flyers.

She approached them and asked, "Why are you young ladies up so early?"

Lolita, the oldest among the girls, giggled, "We're not up early! We've been working since last night!"

Agnes was dumbfounded, "You didn't sleep at all?"

Lolita shook her head, "We've been sleeping all our lives. Now's the time to be awake. It's time to take a new direction in life. Besides, we're really enjoying ourselves."

The other girls chimed in with various comments of agreement. They enthusiastically showed their work to Agnes.

Agnes smiled, "You girls are so hardworking. Let me go get you some breakfast."

The town's enthusiasm was contagious. Everyone was fully committed to the effort and did their best work.

The mountain women started to think and act in unprecedented ways. They introduced innovative business development and sales models. For example, they came up with a micro-retail franchise model to sell and pro-mote their local craft in key cities throughout the country. These micro-retail stores were operated by franchisees in ethnic-looking stalls about the size of a hot dog stand. They were strategically located in malls.

The women also created a multilevel sales channel for their crafts that centered on aggressive sales channels through a network of commission-based agents.

Many of the youth in their mountain village community became involved in the effort. They were able to earn significant income. Some of them were able to save some money for college. Others used the earnings generated to hire people and expand their family's craft business. Others pursued their own new marketing and social media endeavors.

At the year-end meeting of the association members, a much happier mood was evident.

Agnes congratulated the women and their families for their amazing accomplishments. "When we started this movement a year ago," she said, "we were uncertain of the outcome. We wanted to be exporters and go global. We didn't realize that the local market was the key to our success. Our countrymen cared more about our success than others would have. Our products were better appreciated by our local community. Moreover, the local market is a market we know and understand best. The local citizens are also the very people we care about and love. They deserve the very best products we can create."

She paused and looked around the crowded room. A television crew was filming her talk. What a difference a year had made. She continued, "It was not an easy path for us. But our path made a difference in many lives. We have our youth anchored to our culture. We have empowered them to find their own way and fulfill their dreams. Our chosen path not only saved our community but also has become a model of success for our country. Again, congratulations, thank you and more power to all!"

2

UNLINKED, UNWIRED, UNINTERESTED

Each of the featured fictional stories in the preceding chapter offers a lesson in our contemporary global society. While globalization is indeed an economic booster and a developmental pathway for many, others have found their own "economic niches" within a localized setting.

Globalization is not the panacea for all economic and business challenges. It is an important and significant solution pathway, but certainly not the only way.

The "unglobals" in our society have taken an alternative path and have found their own version of success and happiness. They are the "personal" version of economic nationalism that has started to emerge in many parts of the world.

There are important insights that can be gathered from these stories:

Insight 1: Unglobal doesn't mean unhappy. In the case of Alex, the former export and import executive, living in a cave meant freedom and financial independence. In his lifestyle, he uses his time as he pleases. While his chosen path is not easy, he has found his own version of joy and happiness. Being outside the "globalization loop" does not mean one cannot be happy. One merely has to find a simple and viable source of joy and build on it. Minimalist lifestyles and interest in tiny homes has generated much interest in recent years. Many have seen the perils brought about by hyperconsumerism in our society. Many are tired of the rat race and the constant quest for more. Keeping life simple can minimize stress and lead to a happier life. It is a gateway to freedom.

Insight 2: Technological and global withdrawal is tough but doable. The story of John, the tech consultant, underscores the fact that while technology provides an excellent medium for communication and global participation, there can be serious trade-offs. Some would consider a real vacation to mean not having access to mobile phones and the Internet. For others, withdrawal from technology even for a few days would be a real struggle. Technology has become an addiction. A technology-obsessed lifestyle can have adverse effects on family life and business relationships. Finding the right balance between relationships and technology can be beneficial. Lifestyle and operational changes are not easy, but are doable. Weaning oneself off of the overuse of technology on a gradual basis could work well. Creative approaches can make all the difference. Perhaps in the future there will be technology-life balance seminars, technology anonymous organizations, and even tech rehabilitation centers or tech rehabs.

Insight 3: Global skills and abilities are diverse, but need not be connected. The case of Ismael, the deep-sea diver, showcases the fact that there is a diversity of skills in our global society. People have different talents and abilities. All over the world people are leveraging products, services and whatever skills and talents they have in order to support themselves. Many have achieved success by working exclusively within a local context. Globalization certainly offers an excellent pathway to riches and progress. However, it is not the only course to advancement. Working within the framework and ecosystem of a small local community can be economically viable. There are many ways to make a living and to survive. In many cases, these skills and abilities need not be directly linked to the global society at all in order for one to prosper.

Insight 4: Information minimization expands productivity. With the advent of technological advancement and rapid globalization, information overload is far too common. Each day, hours are spent reading useless information and deleting unnecessary e-mails. The story of Jose and Maria, the estate caretakers, shows that one can be productive with very simple information. Selecting and quickly acting on information of value can expand one's productivity. In organizations worldwide, the amount of time wasted by employees on inadequate or unusable information can be mind-boggling. Future technological development needs to be focused on the effective and targeted capture and dissemination of the most relevant information.

Insight 5: Adaptation and innovation come in different forms and shapes. People all over the world are quietly adapting and finding their own groove in a globalized society. The story of the Ecuador mountain women suggests that a localized approach may work for some industries under certain circumstances. In other parts of the world, successful companies have been built by utilizing indigenous products and selling them to the community. Unfortunately, many of these firms did not enjoy full support of the local government and even their communities. Countries need to be more inclusive rather than divisive. The government, alongside local organizations and businesses, should offer support for entrepreneurial adaptations taking place in the community. Harmony in the local ecosystem should be nurtured. Meaningful global citizenship should start at home.

The stories highlight the fact that being unglobal in a globalized society is possible. An unglobal lifestyle and mind-set is often a reflection of an individual or organization's ability to manage five factors: (1) commitment to freedom, (2) technology, (3) skills and competencies, (4) information and knowledge, (5) adaptability and innovation.

Figure 2.1 illustrates the convergence of factors shaping an unglobal mind-set.

The unglobal mind-set means having the courage and intent to try the unconventional. It means breaking away

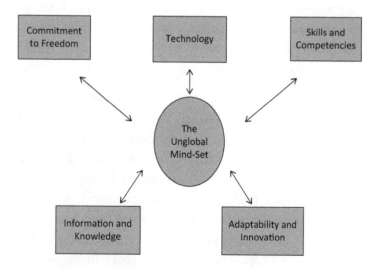

Figure 2.1 The unglobal mind-set

from the norm to define one's own path and destiny. It is about taking charge and being prepared to face new challenges in order to uncover new opportunities. The ability to manage five (5) key factors is essential in the conversion of an unglobal intent into a successful reality. These factors are the following:

1. **Commitment to freedom**. The kind of sacrifices an individual is prepared to make, defines the level of commitment. How far would one go to make a drastic change? The higher the level of commitment, the greater the chances of success. It is important to note that lifetime changes take time. The pursuit of freedom would be associated more closely with a marathon rather than a sprint. In the featured story, Alex was highly committed to change. He also knew he needed significant time and resources to attain his unglobal aspirations.

2. **Technology.** The use of technology in a globalized world should be well balanced. In the fairy tale "Goldilocks and Three Bears," the child Goldilocks prefers her porridge not too hot and not too cold. Individuals and companies need to consider the Goldilocks Way to technology. There shouldn't be too much or too little. Most importantly, it should be well aligned with your goals and objectives. John's approach to technology was strategic in the sense that it provided real value and solutions to family and workplace issues.

3. **Skills and competencies.** Individuals and organizations differ in their skill sets and competencies. In a globalized world, abilities need to be delivered at the right place, at the right time and at the right price. Many

brilliant people in developing nations end up migrating to developed nations during the rise of their careers in order to further grow and to improve their income. Unfortunately, in some nations this has led to a "brain drain." Nevertheless, in some developing nations in the world, those who possess little education, but have a skill to leverage, can find fulfilling and comfortable lives even if they take on an unglobal path. Ismael's best skill was deep-sea diving. With some luck, he found a route to prosperity.

4. **Information and knowledge.** Information is both a boon and a bane to a global society. It is useful in a sense that with instantaneous information at our fingertips, knowledge can be easily acquired and decisions made quickly. For others, information leads to distress and misery. Think about the victims of identity theft and cyberthreats. A minimalist approach can make a difference. In some cases, less Web footprint could mean a lower risk of being a hacker's target. In the story of Jose and Maria, their information-gathering approach is very crude yet functional. They use information solely to suit their needs. With their unglobal lifestyle, they have zero Web footprint. They never have to receive and delete spam e-mail messages every day, and will never be victims of Internet fraud.

5. **Adaptability and innovation**. The ability to adapt and innovate is critical, whether one decides to pursue a global or an unglobal path. More than ever, creative thinking is much appreciated. Leading universities have started to introduce design thinking courses and programs. The Ecuador mountain women were open to change and the implementation of new ideas. For

them adaptation was a practical necessity and a solution pathway. In their story, one thing that was truly commendable was the speed with which plans were executed. Oftentimes, the timing of execution is a key consideration. After all, an exciting innovation implemented late may end up worthless. Innovation comes with an expiration date.

As shown in Figure 2.1, multiple factors need to be considered before one makes the leap to an unglobal lifestyle. Each factor has its own merits and can be a strong decision driver on its own. However, considering all influencing factors altogether can lead to better chances of success.

The featured stories and characters in this book are fictional. However, the scenarios are highly plausible and based on real life stories. There are individuals who are *unlinked*, *unwired* and *uninterested* in globalization. They have a unique mind-set and desire a distinctive lifestyle. They have taken the notion of economic nationalism down to a personal level.

Worldwide, active quests are ongoing for alternative approaches and lifestyles detached from the mainstream. Individuals have started to pursue minimalist lifestyles and even to live in tiny homes as a way of cutting costs and minimizing their carbon footprint. Some have started to take a path toward an unglobal way.

3

UNGLOBAL PATHWAYS

The idea behind this very short book is to stimulate thought and discussion on globalization alternatives and lifestyles. Academic literature and various surveys suggest that globalization has been uneven. It has benefited many, but also alienated others.

The sustainability of globalization is oftentimes questionable. The future is daunting, with global population expected to reach 9.7 billion by 2050, leading to potential constraints on the world's ability to reduce poverty and hunger as well as provide equitable access to basic services, including education and good health care (UNCTAD, 2016).

There is growing multipolarity in a globalized environment requiring clear rules and functional institutions amid a rise in protectionism, currency conflicts and geopolitical discord (Credit Suisse, 2017).

Presently, there seems to be much confusion about globalization. The global citizenry appears perplexed about the extent of globalization. Notably, on the business front a "globaloney" scenario exists, as evidenced by an overestimation of the extent of international versus domestic activities (depth) and an underestimation of the extent to which international activities are globally dispersed (scope) (Ghemawat, 2017).

The shifting and evolving contemporary political, business and economic thinking underscores the fact that new models are necessary. Lund, Manyika and Bughin (2016) noted the growing economic influence of data flows or digital globalization over that of traditional physical goods. Their study underscored the importance of rethinking global footprints, examining value chain changes and alignment of strategies with the digital world, thinking on a large scale and understanding the competitive landscape well.

An open-mindedness toward unglobal pathways may lead to the uncovering of innovative solutions to our society's many pressing challenges. In a PWC (2017) survey of CEOs, only 28 percent believed globalization helps avert climate change and resource scarcity.

Governments need to consider new discussion items on their agenda. For example, policy makers specially in the Western world need to address pressing issues such as inclusiveness of economic growth, the delivery of changes desired by voters while maintaining system continuity in government, and the reconciliation of nationalism movements within diverse societies (World Economic Forum, 2017b). Strategic actions need to be taken to help those affected by trade and globalization, such as (1) reinvestment in communities, (2) enhanced linkages of small firms with international markets, (3) improved access to investors, (4) improved international digital platform connectivity, and (5) a well-conceived platform for the retraining of workers (Pinkus, Manyika and Ramaswany, 2017).

Given the complexity of the global environment, organizations need to think and operate in new and strategic ways. Analytical, innovative and solutions-driven approaches can lead to favorable results. For governments, international organizations and private corporations, the following are recommended:

1. **Assess perceptions toward globalization**. Individuals have divergent views on globalization. Differences in viewpoints can be very pronounced in some organizations. Imagine a company where 70 percent of the employees think globalization is great, and 30 percent absolutely hate it. Execution of plans and strategies can be dampened by disparate attitudes. Assessing perceptions is a good way to start understanding the organization better and planning viable steps forward.

2. **Appoint a committee to explore alternative globalization pathways**. Assembling a core of interested participants to help identify strategic globalization alternatives can open new doors for an organization. Staying open to new and innovative ideas can help create new competitive advantages. A firm can explore game-changing strategies of companies within and outside the firm's industry. An organization can keep fresh ideas flowing continuously in the organization.

3. **Review committee proposals and recommendations**. Committee proposals are best submitted directly to decision makers so that appropriate and timely reviews are made. Radical and game-changing ideas require proper research and due diligence. Organizations can solicit feedback from experts and reliable third parties. They can carefully consider legal and financial consequences.

4. **Implement in stages, starting with the more viable programs first**. Oftentimes drastic and ambitious new programs or strategies require significant organizational changes. The programs may also require large resource commitments. When appropriate, it is best to phase in program implementation. It makes sense to first start with the ones that are easiest to execute. For example, if an organization intends to launch a national "buy local" campaign, implementation can start in one key city first. Progress can be monitored and reviewed. The program can eventually be refined when rolled out to other cities.

5. **Review, evaluate and redesign "reglobalization" programs**. Given that the neoglobal world is constantly evolving, planned programs have to be carefully reviewed and updated. Organizations can plan for future program changes and redesigns in advance. It would be best to create programs that are nimble and flexible. For example, if an organization decides to cease operations in a particular region of the world due to political instability, it should have a reentry strategy ready in case the political environment changes. Opportunities as well as threats can be fleeting in a neoglobal world.

The key questions to ask are shown in Table 3.1.

The chaos, complexity and uncertainty brought about by a neoglobal world sets the stage for experimentation and implementation of creative and strategic approaches. There is a need for everyone to take on an introspective, purposeful and proactive mind-set. For individuals, the following are recommended.

Table 3.1 The unglobal organizational path

Course of action	Key questions
Assess perceptions toward globalization	*How do executives and employees view globalization? Are executives and employees open to alternative globalization approaches? How does globalization impact the corporate bottom line? What are the implications of a change in global strategy? Is the timing right? Are resources available?*
Appoint a committee to explore alternative globalization pathways	*Who should lead the committee to explore globalization alternatives? What is the composition of this committee? What are the committee's goals and responsibilities? What time lines will they follow? What resources are available to them?*
Review committee proposals and recommendations	*Who will review and decide on the committee proposals? Will the reviewers only be internal, or will external reviewers be invited to participate? What are the criteria for evaluation? Who decides on these criteria? What time lines will be followed? What are the legal and financial considerations?*
Implement in stages, starting with the more viable programs first	*What are the priorities for implementation? What time lines need to be considered? Who will take the lead in the implementation? Who will be participating? What resources are necessary?*
Review, evaluate and redesign "reglobalization" programs	*What are the parameters for evaluating and reviewing program success? Who will take the lead in the review process? Who will be participating? How often will reviews and evaluations be conducted? What is the process for program revisions or redesigns?*

1. **Follow your joy and passion**. Being "unglobal" is not for everyone. Happiness is for everyone. Find a career and lifestyle that bring you the greatest level of joy. Gain the courage to pursue this joy, whether it takes you to a global or unglobal path. Alex, the former export-import executive found joy living in a cave. There are many other creative options available.

2. **Redefine technology**. Reassess what technology really means in your life and how it impacts your relationships. Control technology. Don't let it control you. Redefine the essence of technology and manage it well. John, the tech consultant, found a way to manage technology better both at home and in the workplace.

3. **Focus on skills that matter**. Global talent abounds. Given the nature of international competition, develop skills that you can truly excel in. It's not so much the quantity of skills but rather the quality of skills that matters in a neoglobal world. Brainpower is important, but it is not a key indicator to success. Ismael, the deep-sea diver, was not educated at all. His diving skill contributed to his success in a rather "unglobal" way.

4. **Use information on your own terms**. The volume of information global citizens receive everyday is never going to decrease. Instead, the volume of information you receive will increase exponentially in the coming years. Managing information well will help you better manage your time and productivity. There is so much information around the world. An unglobal, or perhaps even a "smart global," strategy is to filter, process and capture the information that offers the highest value. Jose and Maria, the estate caretakers, are extremely

minimalist in the way they gather and use information, yet they manage to live happy and productive lives.

5. **Pursue strategic adaptation and evolution**. Countries and companies regularly update their policies to capture global advantages and steer away from challenges. Individuals should do the same. Strategic global adaptation means going global at times, then becoming unglobal at other times. It also means constantly shifting gears to adapt to an evolving global environment. For example, the Ecuador mountain women may have started out with an "unglobal" strategy. In the years to come, foreign buyers may start to take interest in their craft. An appropriate approach would then be to gradually shift their business development efforts from "local" to "local + international."

The key questions to ask are shown in Table 3.2.

The shared questions in Table 3.2 are by no means complete. They are shown as mere examples of questions to think about as you find your own path toward successful globalization or unglobalization.

In the end, the desired path a person or an organization decides to take is largely anchored on the goals, objectives and situation. Every year a KOF Globalisation Index is reported that measures and ranks countries based on economic, social and political dimensions. In 2017, the top five countries were the Netherlands, Ireland, Belgium, Austria and Switzerland (KOF, 2017).

Given the growing number of discontented people and those seeking alternative approaches, perhaps an unglobalization index should be created. It could measure

Table 3.2 The unglobal personal path

Course of action	Key questions
Follow your joy and passion	*What is your joy and passion? How rooted are you in the globalization lifestyle? Are you prepared to make dramatic changes? Do you have the time, interest and resources to execute unglobal plans? What time lines are you considering? What support will you need?*
Redefine technology	*How extensive a tech user are you? Where does technology really add value to your life and career? Are you prepared to make some changes? In what areas do these changes make the most sense? What impact would these changes have on your life and career?*
Focus on skills that matter	*What are your most valuable skills and competencies? Are these skills best leveraged in a global or local environment? How can you optimize the use of skills and abilities? In what areas can you further grow? What changes can you make and when? What resources do you need?*
Use information in your own terms	*What information is most critical to your life and career? Where can you get this information? How can you optimize the acquisition of needed information? What support do you need? What resources do you need? How can you optimize the use of the gathered information?*
Pursue strategic adaptation and evolution	*In what areas can you further grow? What changes do you need to make? What impact would these changes have? What scenario is best for you— local, global or perhaps both? What resources do you need to be successful? What time lines should you follow?*

economic, social and political detachment from the global community and its implications for countries.

It may also not be a bad idea to forget all indexes altogether and simply measure happiness. The country of Bhutan introduced the notion of Gross National Happiness (GNH), which examines factors such as equitable economic development, environmental preservation, cultural promotion and good governance. The *World Happiness Report* measures country happiness based on factors such as caring, freedom, generosity, honesty, health, income and good governance. The top five countries in the list were Norway, Denmark, Iceland, Switzerland and Finland (*World Happiness Report*, 2017).

Perhaps everyone should be measuring personal global happiness (PGH) and assessing their personal development, environmental harmony, life and cultural appreciation, and relationship to the world.

If each factor had a value of 25 percent, what would your PGH score be? Table 3.3 shows an assessment form that can help you think through factors that impact your personal happiness.

The idea behind the PGH assessment shown in Table 3.3 is simply to help you find your current global bearings. It aims to answer the questions *Where do I really stand within this global society?* and *Am I pleased with where I am?* It will help you identify the factors that make you the happiest and that factors that require change. It is designed simply to help you contemplate and think. It will help you understand your global persona. If you score 75 percent and higher, you are most likely satisfied with where you stand in the broad context of globalization. With a score of 74 percent and below, you may need

Table 3.3 Personal global happiness (PGH) assessment

Factor	Key question	Rating
Personal Development (25%)	*How satisfied are you with your current level of personal development?* (Scale: 0% Highly Unsatisfied to 25% Very Satisfied)	
Environmental Harmony (25%)	*How would you characterize your relationship with nature?* (Scale: 0% Very Poor to 25% Excellent)	
Life and Cultural Appreciation (25%)	*How thrilled are you with your current lifestyle and culture?* (Scale: 0% Not thrilled to 25% Very thrilled)	
Relationship with the World (25%)	*Are you satisfied with your overall current relationships, both as a giver and a receiver?* (Scale: 0% Highly Unsatisfied to 25% Very Satisfied)	

to think about changes that you can make to lead a happier life. It would help to list 5 to 10 key changes you'd like to make, and then plan and prioritize their implementation. Table 3.4 will help you think about possible steps forward.

After you complete your PGH action plan, discuss it with a trusted colleague or loved one and start executing it. Do bear in mind that you may want to review your progress quarterly or semiannually. If a significant other will be impacted by the plan or intends to join you in carrying out the plan, make sure that he or she creates his or her own PGH action plan as well. You can then

Table 3.4 Personal global happiness (PGH) action plan

Planned change	Time line	Resources needed	Projected impact
1.			
2.			
3.			
4.			
5.			
6.			
7.			
8.			
9.			
10.			

reconcile your plans and examine how you can make your plans work well together.

The reality is that you cannot control the path of globalization regardless of whether it is headed uphill or downhill. You cannot control the politics in your country regardless of whether it favors globalization or isolation. You may not even be able to control the strategic direction of your company regardless of whether it intends to globalize or localize. What you can control are your personal actions. You can control your own course and define your destiny in this age of economic nationalism.

The key to your personal global happiness is in your own hands.

The stories and insights in this book point out to alternative pathways and directions as a way of coping with an often chaotic and unpredictable neoglobal world. This is an environment where a dynamic and evolving global economy is influenced by powerful geopolitical and geoeconomic forces. It is a landscape where economic nationalism has captured the imagination of many. It is a society where populist, nationalist or isolationist standpoints are realities in many countries. It is a setting where citizens have the option of living solitary lives and simply mingling within their own miniscule economic ecosystem.

There are several globalization lifestyle options available and numerous directions to take. The featured stories showcase groundbreakers who have taken a different route amid a world of heightened economic nationalism. They are men and women of courage who have defied the norm and dared to pursue the unconventional.

They are the unglobals.

With globalization, the world is indeed your oyster. Given the diversity of talents, interests and values within the global citizenry, some would be perfectly happy to stay the global course, while others might prefer an alternative and unglobal route. Still others might be global in one aspect of their life and unglobal in another area. Yet, still others may shift their mind-set from global to unglobal and vice versa from time to time depending on where the optimum benefit exists. There is no right or wrong approach. However, given your own personal competencies, interests and goals, there is certainly one viable approach that can impact your life and career in a profound way. This may be a route to newfound happiness.

If life has taken you to a fork in the road, the unglobal path could be one to consider.

ABOUT THE AUTHOR

J. Mark Munoz is a tenured full professor of management and international business at Millikin University in Illinois, and a former visiting fellow at the Kennedy School of Government at Harvard University. He is the recipient of several awards, including four Best Research Paper awards, a literary award, an International Book Award, and the ACBSP Teaching Excellence Award among others. Aside from top-tier journal publications, he has authored/edited/coedited 18 books, including *Land of My Birth*, *Winning across Borders*, *A Salesman in Asia*, *International Social Entrepreneurship*, *Handbook on the Geopolitics of Business*, *Advances in Geoeconomics* and *Global Business Intelligence*. As chairman/CEO of the international management consulting firm Munoz and Associates International, he directs consulting projects worldwide in the areas of strategy formulation, business development and international finance.

REFERENCES

Bertelsmann Siftung (2016). *Globalization Report 2016. Who Benefits Most From Globalization?* Accessed December 18, 2017. Available at: https://www.bertelsmann-stiftung.de/fileadmin/files/BSt/Publikationen/GrauePublikationen/NW_Globalization_Report_2016.pdf.

Credit Suisse (2017). "'Getting Over Globalization'—Outlook for 2017." Accessed December 18, 2017. Available at: https://www.credit-suisse.com/corporate/en/articles/media-releases/_getting-over-globalization---what-to-watch-for-in-2017--201701.html.

Dahir, A. L. (2017). "African countries Still Can't Have Enough Capital to Replace Their Bad Roads." Quartz Media. Accessed December 18, 2017. Available at: https://qz.com/945724/african-countries-still-cant-raise-enough-capital-to-fix-their-poor-road-networks/.

Davies, M. (2015). "Average Person Now Spends More Time on Their Phone and Laptop Than Sleeping, Study Claims." *Daily Mail*. Accessed December 15, 2017. Available at: http://www.dailymail.co.uk/health/article-2989952/How-technology-taking-lives-spend-time-phones-laptops-SLEEPING.html.

The Economist (2017). "The World's Most Miserable Countries." Accessed December 18, 2017. Available at: http://www.theworldin.com/edition/2018/article/14460/worlds-most-miserable-countries.

Ghemawat, P. (2017). "Globalization in the Age of Trump." *Harvard Business Review*, July–August. Accessed December 15, 2017. Available at: https://hbr.org/2017/07/globalization-in-the-age-of-trump.

The Guardian (2017). "Japanese Woman 'Dies of Overwork' after Logging 159 Hours of Overtime in a Month," October 5. Accessed December 15, 2017. Available at: https://www.theguardian.com/world/2017/oct/05/japanese-woman-dies-overwork-159-hours-overtime.

HRCI (HR Certification Institute) (2017). "Mixed Expectations about Working while on Vacation Leaves Employees Confused, Finds HR Certification Institute Survey." Accessed December 18, 2017. Available at: https://www.hrci.org/docs/default-source/press-releases/vacation-poll-resultsc9e1228e537e6cd8aac9ff0000 6e5b37.pdf?sfvrsn=6f9f4e61_2).

KOF (2017). KOF Globalisation Index. Accessed December 15, 2017. Available at: http://globalization.kof.ethz.ch/media/filer_public/2017/04/19/rankings_2017.pdf.

Lund, S., Manyika, J., and Bughin, J. (2016). "Globalization Is Becoming More about Data and Less about Stuff." *Harvard Business Review*, March 14. Accessed December 15, 2017. Available at: https://hbr.org/2016/03/globalization-is-becoming-more-about-data-and-less-about-stuff.

Melendez, E. D. (2013). "Financial Crisis Cost Tops $22 Trillion." *HuffPost*, February 14. Accessed December 18, 2017. Available at: https://www.huffingtonpost.com/2013/02/14/financial-crisis-cost-gao_n_2687553.html.

Pinkus, G., Manyika, J., & Ramaswany, S. (2017). "We Can't Undo Globalization But We Can Improve It." *Harvard Business Review*, January 10, pp. 2–5. Accessed: Available at: https://hbr.org/2017/01/we-cant-undo-globalization-but-we-can-improve-it.

Polland, J. (2012). "The Most Vacation Deprived Countries." *Business Insider*, November 16. Accessed December 18, 2017. Available at: http://www.businessinsider.com/which-countries-take-the-least-amount-of-vacation-2012-11

Poushter, J. (2017). "Worldwide, People Divided on Whether Life Today Is Better Than in the Past." Pew Research Center, December 5. Accessed December 18, 2017. Available at: http://www.pewglobal.org/2017/12/05/worldwide-people-divided-on-whether-life-today-is-better-than-in-the-past/.

PWC (2017a). "20 Years inside the Mind of the CEO … What's Next?" Accessed December 15, 2017. Available at: https://www.pwc.com/gx/en/ceo-agenda/ceosurvey/2017/gx.html.

PWC (2017b). "Making Globalization Work for All." Accessed December 15, 2017. Available at: https://www.pwc.com/gx/en/ceo-agenda/ceosurvey/2017/gx/globalisation.html.

Tomita, T. (2017). "Two Myths and Two Realities behind Japan's Support for Globalization," *HuffPost*, August 30. Accessed December 18, 2017. Available at: https://www.huffingtonpost.com/entry/two-myths-and-two-realities-behind-japans-support_us_59a70ba9e4b02498834a8e38.

UNCTAD (United Nations Conference on Trade and Development) (2016). *Development and Globalization: Facts and Figures*. Accessed December 18, 2017. Available at: http://stats.unctad.org/Dgff2016/DGFF2016.pdf.

UNHCR (United Nations High Commissioner for Refugees) (2017). "Figures at a Glance." Accessed December 18, 2017. Available at: http://www.unhcr.org/en-us/figures-at-a-glance.html.

World Atlas (2017). "12 Countries with the Lowest Rates of Cell Phone Subscriptions." Accessed December 18, 2017. Available at: https://www.worldatlas.com/articles/12-countries-with-the-lowest-rates-of-cell-phone-subscriptions.html.

World Bank (2016). "Poverty." Accessed December 15, 2017. Available at: http://www.worldbank.org/en/topic/poverty/overview.

World Economic Forum (2017a). *Global Risks Report 2017*. 12th ed. Accessed December 18, 2017. Available at: http://www3.weforum.org/docs/GRR17_Report_web.pdf.

World Economic Forum (2017b). *Social and Political Challenges*. Accessed December 15, 2017. Available at: http://reports.weforum.org/global-risks-2017/part-2-social-and-political-challenges/2-1-western-democracy-in-crisis/.

World Happiness Report (2017). *World Happiness Report*. Accessed December 15, 2017. Available at: http://worldhappiness.report/wp-content/uploads/sites/2/2017/03/HR17.pdf.

YouGov (2016). International Survey: Globalization Still Seen as a Force of Good in the World. Accessed December 15, 2017. Available at: https://today.yougov.com/news/2016/11/17/international-survey/.

Printed in the USA
CPSIA information can be obtained
at www.ICGtesting.com
LVHW041245070824
787596LV00002B/22

9 781785 270550